Master Churches

Master Churches

Strategies for Reformation

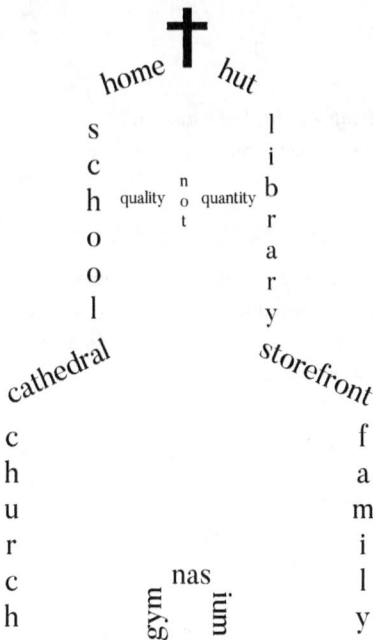

home hut

school quality not quantity library

cathedral storefront

church gymnasium family

Church is people NOT a Place

Kirby Clements Sr.

CLEMENTS MINISTRIES
Decatur, GA

Master Churches: Strategies for Reformation

Address inquiries to the publisher:

Clements Family Ministries
2000 Cathedral Place
Decatur, Georgia 30034 USA

Learn more about the authors and their ministry at
www.clementsministries.org

ISBN: 978-0-9968702-8-3 (Print)
ISBN: 978-0-9968702-9-0 (Ebook)

LCCN: 2020912573

Editor: Annette Johnson with Annyce Stone

Printed in the United States of America

Dedication

To the Community of the Holy Spirit

About the Author

My wife, Sandra, and I entered the ministry in the 1970s during the Charismatic and Word of Faith emphasis. It was a time when ethnic and racial barriers were being lowered and the "browning" of churches was a new integration phenomenon due to Blacks and Whites worshipping together. There was a focus upon worship, unity, evangelism, local church, episcopacy, racial and denominational reconciliation, restoration of those who were estranged and fallen, and even church buildings. Sandra and I were pastors at one of the first megachurches in America. The Cathedral of the Holy Spirit was a vibrant congregation of over 12,000 members, 24 pastors and over 400 deacons and caregivers from different racial, ethnic and cultural backgrounds. We combined preaching, teaching, ministration of the Holy Ghost, a structure of elders, deacons and caregivers, innovative worship using drama, arts, hymns, gospel, rock, rap, and contemporary music, and some very effective strategies for shepherding and evangelism. We provided oversight to leaders and ministries throughout the United States, Asia, Africa, Australia, Caribbean, Europe, Latin, and Central America.

We witnessed every dimension of church life with all of its privileges, challenges, victories, and even failures. It is a faithful saying that until we comprehend the reasons and implications of the finished work of Jesus Christ and the various dimensions of the Kingdom of God, we will struggle over the identity, mission, and work of the Church. The presence and ministry of the Holy Ghost, along with sound doctrinal beliefs and practices, are indispensable for healthy and productive church life. We were privileged to serve for over 30 years and to write many books on church structure, the co-equality of men and women, prophetic ministry, discernment, spiritual intelligence, faith, Kingdom of God, and other aspects of church life. Sandra and I co-labored together in ministry, dentistry and every aspect of life for nearly 50 years.

Contents

About the Author, vii

1. A Proposition 1
2. A Redemptive Idea 5
3. Historical Overview 7
4. Models of the Church 11
5. The Building of a People 13
   - Character 16
   - Intelligence 17
   - Truth 19
   - Power 20
6. Indispensable Perspective 21
7. Comprehensive Preaching 23
8. Neglected Emphasis: The Resurrection 29
9. Neglected Emphasis: The Person and Ministry of the Holy Spirit 37
10. Comparing Spiritual with Spiritual 41
11. Reformations, Fads and Times of Refreshing 43
    - Reformations 43
    - Fads 45
    - Times of Refreshing 46
12. Historical Warnings and Observations 49

Summary 59

Other Books by the CFM 60

CHAPTER 1

A PROPOSITION

The Church is people and not place. Thus, it cannot be defined by any geographic location or physical structure. In addition, the Church is quality of people and not quantity. Thus, it is not defined by the numbers of people in any place or at any time. The Church represents those who have been spiritually and psychologically re-engineered by grace to know God and make Him known.

Similarly, salvation is the process by which God takes the sinner from depravity to ultimate destiny. Salvation as a comprehensive work is spiritual, psychological, and behavioral. In fact, salvation is a comprehensive word into which other words must fit, such as regeneration, sanctification, imputation, and restoration. Salvation provides privileges and responsibilities irrespective of gender, race, socioeconomic status, and age.

The Church and the Kingdom of God are distinct but inseparable. The Kingdom of God is the defining concept that influences the attitude and operational behavior of the Church. The Kingdom must be viewed in its comprehensive identity as past, present, future, heavenly, earthly, spiritual, and natural. The Kingdom relates to laws, legislation, and government while the Church is associated with congregations, meetings, and worship. Thus, the Kingdom is in the Holy Ghost while the Church is the residential community of the Holy Ghost.

The Holy Ghost is the executive administrator of the Kingdom and mediates all heavenly/earthly interactions. The Holy Ghost is received as power and not intelligence. The intelligence of the Kingdom is to be found in the Scriptures. While the Holy Ghost enables the renewal of the minds of believers, the Holy Ghost does not inform their minds intellectually. Consequently, the presence of the Holy Ghost in the life of the believer is no substitute for sound doctrines and beliefs. The relationship between the Spirit and the Word is most significant since all Word and no Spirit is dead intellectuality, and all Spirit and no Word results in fanaticism.

Evangelism is the comprehensive process by which God takes the sinner and creation from depravity to ultimate destiny. It is the spiritual and psychological re-engineering of people and the organizations, laws, and institutions associated with their existence. Evangelism is comprehensive and includes soul winning, church planting, and cultural transforming. While the salvation of the individual may be the center of Divine will, it is not the circumference, for we know the scriptures say the earth shall be filled with the glory of the Lord. Hence, evangelism is comprehensive and involves the creature and all creation.

If these statements are true, then the nature of the worship space, congregation size, financial base, geographic location, and leadership skills may not be the determining factors for the effectiveness of the Church. Since the Church as a redemptive community is a spiritual and natural entity, perhaps the source of its authority and influence may need some re-clarification. Perhaps the most significant factors may be the ability to get answers to prayers, receive and communicate Divine information, obey Divine directives, and integrate Divine truths and practices into the world. Relevance, effectiveness and influence may reside in a different set of factors. If the world is viewed in a moral sense as people, institutions, organizations, wisdom, knowledge, values, and priorities in opposition to Divine authority, then the significant factors of the world's influence may include specific powers, authority, information, and behavior patterns proclaimed and demonstrated by the Church community.

Leadership is critical in the initiation, development, and ongoing work of a ministry. Likewise, the work, character, and competence of the congregation is indispensable. The ethics, moral values, and willingness of the people to accomplish the mission of worship, prayer, evangelism, restoration, reconciliation, healing, and reformation is indispensable. While leaders are called to equip the saints for this work of the ministry, the mission and work of the Church is a shared responsibility. Furthermore, relationship between leadership and congregation is influenced by concepts of the Kingdom of God and the Church. There can be leadership-dependent and leadership-interdependent congregations. The distinction resides in the development of the priesthood of the believers alongside the emphasis on leadership capabilities.

Congregation relationship is significant. Since contemporary congregations have a variety of histories, including Protestant, Roman Catholic, Pentecostal, Charismatic, and atheistic, the ability to orient a plural group around some common purposes, priorities, and perspectives is a challenge to be addressed. The ultimate goal of their unity must be greater than their individual differences. Congregational synergy is the ability of a group to integrate sociological differences such as race, age, socioeconomic status, and gender into a functional and cooperative community. Congregational literacy is not simply knowledge of doctrines and disciplines but the ability to un-learn and re-learn redemptive truths, practices, and priorities when traditions become contradictions.

There are churches that will serve as models of these propositions. They will influence the attitude and behavior of other churches. In this book, they are referred to as "master churches." Like Noah, during a time of tremendous spiritual and moral decline, these churches will serve as curators of redemptive truths, values, objectives, priorities, and practices. Their effectiveness and relevance will reside in their prayers, revelation and obedience to Divine directives.

CHAPTER 2

A REDEMPTIVE IDEA

The authority of the church rests upon its origin, and its influence resides in its privilege to get answers to prayers, receive and communicate Divine information, and to obey the Lord in totality. Consequently, the nature of the worship space, congregation size, financial base, geographic location, and leadership skills may not be the determining factors for success. Instead, the most significant factors may be the ability to integrate Divine information and practices into the world. If the world is viewed in a moral sense as people, institutions, organizations, wisdom, knowledge, values, and priorities in opposition to Divine authority, then the significant factors may include the ability to spiritually and psychologically re-engineer people and the world.

This book seeks to explore the idea of redeemed communities known for their impact and influence. They will not be known necessarily by the congregation size, worship space, economic abilities, and other such characteristics. In fact, they may meet in rented spaces, houses, schools, and even traditional structures. The congregation, staff, and budgets will be smaller, but they will effectively merge their preaching and teaching agendas with the ministration of the Holy Spirit. Their government will be a functional plurality of elders with strong emphasis on the priesthood of believers. They will demonstrate the co-equality of men and women, regardless of their race, culture or ethnicity, in order to serve in every aspect of ministry, home, and even the market place. Evangelism will focus on winning souls, planting churches, and transforming cultures. Worship will be a prophetic re-enactment of historic truths, events, and practices.

They will blend the psalms, hymns, spiritual songs, gospels, and contemporary music with drama and the arts. These churches will influence the attitude and operational behavior of other churches and ministries regardless of their doctrinal and practical differences. Since relevance and popularity are not synonymous, these ministries will effectively integrate Divine purposes, principles, practices, and perspective despite the challenges of their communities.

Ultimately, these churches will be known as "master churches" because of their impact and influence on the world. During a time of spiritual and moral demise, they will be viewed as curators of truths, practices, and values that must be received, restored, and transmitted into a present world.

CHAPTER 3

HISTORICAL OVERVIEW

This past century has witnessed tremendous charismatic activities as expressed in revival emphasis on such topics as the Kingdom of God, church growth, prayer, unity, reconciliation, restoration, faith, supernatural, evangelism, church structure, apostolic and prophetic ministry, eschatology, five-fold ministry, priesthood of believer, worship, evangelism, and other areas. The charismatic dimension of the Church made its entrance into the market places, homes, and even political spheres through media, technology and study groups. In addition, reconciliation movements challenged the restrictive distinctions of race, gender, nationality and even socio-economic status. Creative and innovative strategies in evangelism and public worship introduced the arts and a variety of musical expressions. As a result, worship campuses evolved to accommodate growing congregations.

Ultimately, the emphasis on the Kingdom of God greatly influenced the attitude and operational behavior of the churches toward the world. An escape-theology was replaced with a theology of influence. Technology and social media made the worship experience available to a broader audience. The "cyber church" and the "virtual reality church" provided convenience of a worship experience without being physically present. However, the relevance of local churches was measured by their popularity and compliance with the demands, expectations, and norms of the world they were desperately trying to influence. Relevance and popularity became synonymous. Intellectual communities sprung up that provided information but lacked the power so evident in the early Church. In fact, an anti-charismatic sentiment evolved in many churches due to an overemphasis on success, church structure, and growth. Congregations exhibited a mixture of different racial, ethnic, generational, and socioeconomic groups, but the emphasis upon the leadership function of the churches also diminished the activities of the priesthood of believers. Ministry success was measured by size of congregations, nature of the worship space, technology, the communication skills of the leaders, and the financial strengths. Moreover, churches that did not exhibit such standards were viewed as marginal and even failures.

There was a Divine response to this spiritual and psychological climate in the form of a reformation. There were gradual revival emphases that seemed to refocus the work and mission of the Church. As the Holy Spirit sparked the initiation of new ministries and even a revival of old ones, there seemed to be a reformation of clarity at hand. As a result, the focus of this reclarification was theology, sociology, structure, evangelism, and worship.

* **Theology** explored the way Scriptures were viewed and the doctrines and practices created.

* **Sociology** revealed the intramural activities of local redeemed communities when they came together for worship.

* **Structure** examined the ecclesiastical offices, priesthood of the believer and governmental relationships.

* **Evangelism** uncovered the deficiency of churches to reach the world.

* **Worship** examined historical and contemporary ingredients and patterns of corporate gatherings to determine Biblical normalcy.

There were model churches that proclaimed and demonstrated changes in all of these areas. One such church was the Cathedral of the Holy Spirit in Decatur, Georgia. It was the first megachurch known around the world for its Kingdom theology, governmental structure, evangelistic strategies, youth ministry, schools, excellent musical expressions, dramatic presentations, integrated congregation, and the massive neo-gothic sanctuary. It hosted regular conferences to demonstrate its doctrine, as well as the internal and external activities that received a global audience. It once served as a model to be emulated by other churches. In fact, prior to scandals that contributed to its demise, it became a master church in its ability to influence attitude and operational behavior of other churches throughout the world.

Another model church is the Community of the Holy Spirit in Decatur, Georgia. This is a house church with a small congregation known for its teachings, media presentations, weekly discussion sessions, and ministration of the Holy Spirit. It hosts an annual conference that attracts hundreds of leaders and people from Africa, Asia, Australia, Europe, South and Central America and the United States. Its ability to influence other churches and ministries resides in its publications, emphasis on ministration of the Holy Spirit, practical teaching , and ability to attract and influence the many visitors that come through the ministry to receive teaching and spiritual ministry.

As aforementioned, this work sets forth a reformation strategy called master churches. Fundamentally, these churches are Biblically normal churches. They will not necessarily be known by their congregation sizes, worshipping spaces, financial capabilities, or even their visibility or popularity. Their effectiveness will reside in their willingness and abilities to receive answers to prayers, receive and communicate Divine information, and totally obey the Lord. Many of them will fellowship in smaller facilities with smaller congregations and staffs. Their relevance will depend upon their integration of Divine purposes, priorities, perspectives, and values into their surrounding cultures. Because of their beliefs, ministry efforts, and strategies to influence their communities, they will be known as cultural architects, not cultural critics, that will spiritually and psychologically re-engineer their world.

CHAPTER 4

MODELS OF CHURCH

In keeping with our concept of master churches that influence the attitude and operational behavior of other churches, a brief review of other models is interesting. There have been numerous models of the churches inspired by Biblical characters such as Abraham, Noah, Moses, Joseph, Joshua, Nehemiah, and David. Some were crafted around concepts of faith and mission endeavors. In an effort to be relevant and contemporary, there arose "eclectic" and "hybrids" models which sought to integrate concepts of business, entertainment, spirituality, and trendy technology into the worship experience. Each model sought to address contemporary issues in society with Biblically-based principles, practices, and concepts. In the process of change, the tension always rested in the issues of continuity and discontinuity. That is, in the quest for the new and the different, there has always been the challenge to discern beliefs, practices, and values that are timeless from those that were timely.

The following is a brief overview of some models of the Church:

1. **Noah model:** a crisis is at hand and God desires to deliver His people from these cataclysmic events. This is a model of preservation.
2. **Abraham model:** an exploration and movement into new dimension

3. **Faith model:** the confession of victory not yet seen and receiving what is not yet given
4. **Joseph model:** centers on the significance of a vision and prospering in a strange land through foresight, discernment, transcendence and character
5. **Moses model:** a deliverance journey toward a promised dimension revealing the providential aspect of God, miracles, signs and wonders
6. **Joshua model:** a militant and warfare model that drives out the enemy and includes an understanding the incarnation of evil in systems, structures, organizations, laws, legislation etc.
7. **Unity of the Saints model:** provides for unity, diversity and oneness along with ecumenical strategies to develop cooperation and dialogue
8. **Nehemiah model:** calls for restoration of communities, cities, beliefs and practices
9. **David model:** stresses dominion, rule and restoration that has impact and influence upon sociopolitical and religious structures, values, beliefs and expressions
10. **Eclectic model:** a hybrid and mixture of different ingredients of faith. This is a difficult model, for it must comprehend continuity/discontinuity and essential truth while not sacrificing fundamental values and practices for the sake of cultural relevance and popularity.

These models represented efforts to identify and revive certain specific ministry functions of the Church. None represented a comprehensive function but serves to reveal some of the reformation strategies that influenced the attitude and behavior of many ministries.

CHAPTER 5

THE BUILDING OF A PEOPLE

In this chapter, we will discuss some critical characteristics of an effective congregation. While congregations are common in most churches, we will examine this concept from a master church perspective.

A congregation is a gathering or collection of people obeying some common religious rule. Generally, they are characterized by their common beliefs, testimonies, conversations, values, objectives, priorities, musical preferences, place of gathering ,and other social similarities such as food, clothing, etc. In contemporary culture, there may be a lack of common histories since congregation members emerge from every kindred, tribe, and tongue. In many instances, race is not always a viable factor to define the culture of a congregation, for within the same race there are significant variations defined by geography, socio-economics, education, and sociopolitical distinctions.

The character of a congregation relates to it moral and ethical values. The members' competence is defined by their spiritual intelligence and level of dependence upon leadership. There are leadership-dependent and leadership-interdependent congregations based upon the degree of emphasis on priesthood of the believer. An overemphasis on leadership, authority, and structure can limit the work of a congregation. When the work of the ministry is viewed as a leadership function only, then the congregation becomes passive and unusually reliant upon the leadership for direction, motivation, and even discernment.

A congregation of people from different racial, cultural, socioeconomic , and ethnic backgrounds can lack unity if there is not a vision or focus greater than their individual differences. In essence, different kinds of people gathering together does not comprise a congregation. There must be the development of a common objective that will transcend all of the historical differences of the people.

Discernment is critical to a congregation. Since the work of the church is the work of the congregation, there is the necessity of knowing how, what, and when. The ability to determine times, seasons, and proper response is critical. In essence, there must be the development of a spiritual intelligence that empowers people with a working understanding of their salvation. It is critical to understand the beliefs, values, attitudes, and behavioral patterns necessary for effective priesthood.

As earlier noted, Church is a people and not a place. It is quality of people and not necessarily quantity. Paul declares that God does not dwell in temples made with hands (Acts 17:24-28). Peter refers to this temple as a "spiritual house," "lively stones," and a "holy priesthood" (1 Pet. 2:5). These people are the products of information, values, needs, expectations, and objectives. From a Biblical perspective, the creation motif is the basis of congregation, for it reveals a people made in the image of God. While the term "congregation" is not used in the creation story, there is the reality of a people responding to Divine person, presence, and revelation.

" Congregation," therefore, is the idea of Israel as a holy nation and a peculiar people identified by a covenant that determines every aspect of their existence. Their covenant with God defines their ethical and moral values, interpersonal relationships, and their identity in the world of different nations. Historically, in Jewish culture the three words that define congregation are cabal, edah, and mowed. "Cabal" refers to the ethnic Israelite and excludes any mixed multitude. "Edah" is a whole assembly of both Israelite and a mixed multitude. "Mowed" is an assembly inclusive of everyone such as Israelites and non-Israelites. Historically, the Jews were non-conformist to the world and hyper-ethnocentric in beliefs, dress, mannerism, behavior, food, and other cultural patterns. The word "peculiar," then means to belong to God, for all of these descriptions make this people His unique people. Noteworthy of the Jewish people was the moral and spiritual intelligence of the congregation that was totally determined by their compliance to the Law.

Our contemporary redeemed communities consist of people out of many different races, nations, cultures, and ethnic groups. While the congregation may experience a common salvation, their previous social and religious experiences are varied. When they come together, they rarely discard their traditions and core values. Patterns of social behavior expressed in food, clothing, marriage, funerals, music, and responses in the worship climate are not always abandoned. The doctrines and traditions that shaped the attitude and behavior of the former Baptist, Methodist, Episcopalian, Pentecostal, Roman Catholic, Charismatic, and Independent are rarely discarded. The spiritual and psychological re-engineering of a mixed congregation is a redemptive process accomplished through preaching, teaching, seminars, group meetings, orientation sessions, and public worship experiences. The ability to un-learn and re-learn is the crisis factor.

CHARACTER

The character of a congregation relates to the ethical and moral values. Character is defined by dependency and interdependency upon leadership. Since the word becomes flesh, leaders can condition the dependency level of a congregation. An overemphasis upon leadership identity and development at the expense of the priesthood of the believer is a dangerous proposition. A proper understanding of the mission and coming of Jesus is the indispensable marker.

Congregational character is demonstrated in a personal survey that I devised to examine the reasons for the growth of the Cathedral of the Holy Spirit. During the most significant growth phase of the ministry, I surveyed our congregation that was well over 10,000 people from different races, ethnic groups, nations, ages, and socioeconomic groups. I sought to discover the reason why they were coming to the church and even recommending others to join them. The reasons for their coming revealed their concepts of church. The following represents a brief summation:

*proximity of the church to their home
*preaching content and style
*music, drama, and arts program
*the church activities and social programs
*physical facilities (a newly built neo-gothic Cathedral)
*availability of counsel and pastoral care
*guest speakers and musicians
*public popularity of the ministry
*the diverse congregation
*acceptance of mixed racial marriage
*youth and children programs

These reasons, although not exhaustive, revealed perceptions of the church that were highly social. Attending a service at the Cathedral was transforming to them. The theology, sociology, worship, evangelism, and even the structure were attractive and informative . They professed to experience a Divine encounter regardless of their age, socioeconomic status, and even their religious histories. The sense of a Divine encounter was due to Christ-centered worship that included historic and contemporary musical selections. There was ministry for them from the cradle to the grave! And the content and style of the preaching and teaching developed a love, compassion, and concern for others regardless of their social backgrounds. They saw themselves as spiritual and practical producers, and not simply consumers. The priesthood of the believer was most prominent and actionable among the congregation. Moreover, the people did the work of evangelism, prayer, healing, deliverance, and shepherding. In essence, they were not leadership-dependent but more leadership-interdependent. While there existed a clear distinction between the identity and function of the leaders and the congregation, the congregation saw themselves as salt, light, and influencers.

INTELLIGENCE

Once again, spiritual intelligence is the concept that defines the competence and character of the congregation to accomplish the mission of the church in worship, prayer, evangelism, restoration, reconciliation, deliverance, and discernment. Spiritual intelligence is the defining term and identifies the ability of the congregation to understand the redemptive process and all of its implications, privileges, and responsibilities. It is the ability of the congregation to influence the external environment. The high level of competence was directly related to the preaching/teaching content and the presence of educational opportunities that provided training in various areas of life.

There are perhaps three strategies to influence human behavior.

> First, there is the external imposition of laws that influence behavior by reason of consequences.
>
> Second, there is internal regeneration by the salvation process that transforms the entire individual. This is especially true when salvation is viewed as spiritual, psychological and behavioral.
>
> Third, there is the incarnation of ideas, beliefs and information which greatly influence the attitude and behavior.

With these strategies in mind, consider carefully that words become flesh once they are believed, internalized, and acted upon. We live in an age where technology has made censored and uncensored information readily available. Statistics have been used to influence public opinion regarding the character, identity and relevance of the Church. Publications and media presentations have sought to question the integrity of Scripture, dismiss the reality of absolute truths and question the identity and finished work of Jesus Christ.

People begin to misbehave when their faith propositions are challenged and their internal world of beliefs and expectations are in contradiction to their external environment. They cease to gather for worship and do the work of evangelism because of their doubts, concerns, misconceptions and even disappointments. Whenever the redeemed community ceases to retain a Biblical knowledge of the ways of life in the Kingdom of God, then they cease to be salt and light. Leaders who desire their congregations to become master churches should discern these challenges and equip the congregation with the knowledge, wisdom, and discernment necessary to navigate the issues of life.

TRUTH

The battleground within the Church as a whole has always been doctrinal. Master churches must seek to find the whole truth within God's word, carefully examining the scriptures beyond traditions, but also remaining within the God's character and His Word. For example, the interpretation and misinterpretation of historical truths and practices can influence the attitudes and behaviors of people. This has been true concerning functional relationship between men and women in the church, home, and market place. Although the initial intention of God in creation establishes the co-equality of men and women, misconceptions of words such as authority, submission, and covering have put women and even families at risk. While there is no Biblical precedent to suggest that gifts, callings, and privileges are awarded based upon gender, misinterpretation of the creation narrative in Genesis 1-3 has generated a male-dominated hierarchy in the church, home, and even market place.

When people cease to believe properly, then they cease to behave properly. Doubt, suspicion, and skepticism among a congregation are often the consequence of challenges in areas of health, finance, relationship, education, and personal concerns. Unrealistic expectations and personal disappointments must be managed, for they will masquerade themselves in the attitude and behavior of a congregation. Master churches address these issues effectively with information and integrity.

POWER

Diminished emphasis on the person and ministry of the Holy Spirit has created intellectual communities lacking Pentecostal power that was so evident in the early churches. Churches are often strong in preaching, teaching, and doctrine but weak in spiritual ministration. Or they are strong in the latter and weak in the former. The Kingdom of God is in Word and Power. Whenever and wherever the Church has been most effective, or in master level ability, there has been an emphasis on the person and ministry of the Holy Spirit. It is impossible to produce a spiritual ministry without spiritual resources. The work of the Holy Spirit through the spiritual gifts and callings among the saints is indispensable for effective ministry.

Master churches must have the people with that characteristic along with the following:

*__Discernment:__ knowing times and season and ability to give clarity
*__Foresight:__ understanding the future and appropriate responses
*__Persuasiveness:__ ability to precipitate trust in their presence
*__Transcendence:__ willingness to communicate across natural borders of race, age, socioeconomic and gender
*__Integrity:__ demonstrating charisma and character
*__Spirit Dynamic:__ the power to influence the natural
*__Global Awareness:__ conscious of the world beyond the borders of religion
*__Compassion:__ the skills to comfort a hurting world
*__Longevity:__ demonstrating persistence, endurance and effectiveness
*__Consistency:__ exhibiting dependability and reliability

CHAPTER 6

INDISPENSABLE PERSPECTIVES

Perspective is the picture we paint of life. It is akin to a worldview and expresses values, objectives, strategies, and beliefs. There are some perspectives that are indispensable for the work of master churches:

1. **Full counsel:** avoidance of over specialization or marginalization of the Gospel and embracing the comprehensive Kingdom of God
2. **Transcendence:** communication across borders of race, age, gender, socioeconomic status and religious orientations
3. **Consistency:** maintaining the essence of the message and mission of faith while embracing healthy trends and cycles, not "bouncing back and forth"
4. **Long range:** conscious of the future while being aware of historical implications (landmarks and visions)
5. **Endurance:** finishing the course, self-rehabilitation, being persuaded and managing challenges and contradictions

These perspectives are indispensable for a productive life. They represent concepts of thinking and provide a framework for making decisions. Perspectives represent the pictures we paint of life and they can be used to endorse the values, objectives and priorities we seek to establish. The master churches will be mindful of these.

CHAPTER 7

COMPREHENSIVE PREACHING

Master churches understand the depth of the Gospel message. The Gospel is the power of God unto salvation. It is the setting forth of Divine purposes, priorities, requirements, and values. It also reveals God as Creator, Organizer, and Maintainer of all creation. The Gospel sets forth the propositions that humanity is made in the image of God and endowed with such capacities as creativity, dominion, righteousness, rationality, and communality. The Gospel reveals what went wrong, the deception of humanity, and the consequences. Furthermore, the Gospel uncovers the comprehensive Divine plan of restoration through Christ Jesus which is salvation.

Salvation is the comprehensive process by which God takes the sinner and creation from depravity to ultimate destiny. While individual salvation may be the center of God's will, it is not the circumference. For we know the scriptures declare the earth is to be filled with the glory of the Lord. The Gospel reveals the privileges and responsibilities of this restoration. It also reveals the nature and character of God; Divine involvement in human affairs; strategies for human response; and the objectives and priorities of this grace.

Salvation should also be understood and preached as spiritual, psychological and behavioral.

***The spiritual dimensio**n speaks of the exchange on the Cross where the Father placed upon His Son, Jesus Christ, the punishment and consequences of the sin of all creation. Jesus became sin so that we could become righteous.

***The psychological dimension** of this salvation relates to our acceptances and comprehension of this fact.

***The behavioral dimension** demonstrates the beauty of this salvation being expressed in the attitude and behavior of the believer.

Evangelism is a strategy of spreading the Gospel of salvation and has always been soul winning, church planting, and cultural transforming. Through the evangelistic efforts of congregations and master churches, God fills the earth with the knowledge of His glory. Hence, preaching should stress the redemptive and providential dimensions of God to save and rule. Comprehensive preaching sets forth the stewardship responsibility of redeemed humanity to create civilizations and cultures that demonstrate the righteous rule of God in all areas of life. Master churches will proclaim the fact that there is no boundary line between the sacred and the secular where God is restricted to the former. Such preaching will avoid a marginalization of the Gospel and an overspecialization of aspects of the redemptive package. That is, the preaching will not limit its content to individual privileges but will also include individual responsibilities in the stewardship of all creation.

Ultimately, it is God's will to have a spiritually and psychologically re-engineered people who will be stewards of His creation. This kind of Church results from the preaching of Jesus and His redemptive sacrifice and its setting forth of the presence and implication of the comprehensive Kingdom of God. Master churches will grasp that concept in a holistic sense and understand that what the Cross ended, the Resurrection began. Furthermore, the resurrection authorized Pentecost, which inaugurated the Church as the agent of salvation. And it is wonderful to know that these re-engineered people have no generational curses and have been delivered from evil and empowered with righteousness. Moreover, they will exert influence in all the spheres of human endeavors, such as education, science, economics, entertainment, politics, religion, athletics, and etc.

Master churches will understand and stress the privilege and necessity of believers to get answers to prayers, receive Divine information, and totally obey the Lord. They will demonstrate prayer as a dialogue and not a monologue where only the believer speaks and God listens. They will additionally discern between Divine liability and human responsibility. The former reveals what God will do and the latter uncovers the responsibility of the believer in getting answers to prayers. Master churches will proclaim and demonstrate the benefits of receiving revelation knowledge about Divine purposes, priorities, and perspectives regarding the life of the believer and the creation. Also, master churches will demonstrate the blessings of obedience and the consequences of disobedience to the Lord.

Sometimes in our efforts to be relevant, we dress the Gospel with social, intellectual, and psychological content in order to reach the mind of the intellectual sinner. However, it is neither intellectual reasoning nor psychological content that will convert the sinner. In some places, preaching is being replaced with drama, arts, and music. These activities have their place, but they are not a substitute for preaching Jesus, for the message He preached is set forth as the central focus of the Gospel message. He did not preach about Himself, but rather He preached the Kingdom of God. Nonetheless, we must be clear of Jesus

Christ as presented in the Scripture. It is not the Jesus in the manger, on the Cross or in the tomb, but it is the resurrected Christ seated at the right hand of power. It is Jesus to whom all power and authority has been given.

Christianity can also be seen and preached as a propositional faith and there are fundamental beliefs that must be declared, believed, and acted upon. Some of these propositions include the deity of Jesus; the reality of sin; the necessity of spiritual regeneration; the inspiration of Scripture; the resurrection of Jesus; the privilege of prayer; and the responsibility of evangelism. These and other faith propositions will be embraced, proclaimed, and demonstrated by master churches. In addition, master churches will see, from a Biblical perspective, where the preaching of the Gospel is authenticated by power, signs, and wonders. It has been somewhat of a popular opinion to believe that such validations are either waned or that they are restricted to field evangelism in other nations. It is thought that where the Gospel has been heard and believed, there is no need for the authentication of its power. There is no Biblical validation for such a negative view of the whole gospel. Signs and wonders should be expected and expressed through the gifts of the Holy Spirit working through leaders and the people, who will be found in the master churches.

Something more is to be said about the content and intent of preaching. Whenever the word "preach" is used in Scripture, the focus is Christ, Gospel, Word or Kingdom. The intent of preaching is to stir the emotions, inform the mind, and command the will. According to Paul, the content of preaching should include knowledge, revelation, doctrine, and prophecy. Knowledge is information gained through experience; revelation is Divine disclosure of truths, priorities and purposes; doctrine is interpretation and practical application of the

Scripture; and prophecy is the implication of the person and ministry of the Holy Spirit (gifts). Knowledge may include contemporary information, as well as psychological and sociological content, but doctrine is most essential. While the message can be structured with wide-ranging contemporary insights and understanding, these foundational thoughts ought to be considered, particularly by master churches, for the sake of full balance.

To conclude, the Gospel contains concepts, propositions, revelations, strategies, and demands. It is a comprehensive message that speaks of heavenly, earthly, spiritual, natural, temporal, and eternal matters. Furthermore, it gives meaning to the comprehensive nature of a Kingdom-oriented salvation that is both individual and cosmic. Master churches offer the Gospel in a holistic manner that sets forth the nature of redemption, sanctification, regeneration, justification, imputation, and reconciliation. They preach a comprehensive message that outlines the process by which the Lord brings the sinner and all creation from depravity to ultimate destiny. Once again, the message is validated by a heavenly witness. This validation by the supernatural is timeless, transcendent, and not limited to nations, physical buildings, days of the week, times of the year, or any natural construction. It is neither limited to a specifically designated "evangelism time," nor is it delegated to occur only when a certain speaker appears. Signs are to follow those who believe, and those who believe are both leaders and followers. This is the preaching from master churches that produces spiritual and psychological architects and engineers of our world.

CHAPTER 8

NEGLECTED EMPHASIS: The Resurrection

As we continue our discussion of master churches, there is a critical topic to be considered. We hear the word "resurrection" often used as a synonym defining new life, victory over death, success out of devastation, and even a new opportunity or second chance. However, it is a spiritual word used with great clarity in the Christian faith since the Resurrection is one of the foundation stones of faith.

If Christ be not raised then our preaching is in vain and our faith is also useless and we be false witnesses for we have testified that God did raise up Christ. And if the dead do not rise then Christ is not risen and our faith is futile and we are yet in our sins. But Christ is raised and is the first fruit of those who have fallen to sleep (1 Cor. 15:12-20).

The Crucifixion speaks of the cost of our salvation while the Resurrection testifies to the power. Yet, in our contemporary world, the concept of resurrection is tossed around quite frequently in secular circles. News media commentators and political spokespersons use the term in their reports. The comeback of a celebrity; the career turnaround of an athlete; the reinstatement of a displaced politician; the recovery of the stock market; a new image for an old industry; the reconciliation of an estranged political alliance; and other instances are often spoken of in association with the word resurrection. When used in the sociological context, resurrection is always preceded by a seemingly impossible turn of events or the prognosis of death. Therefore, as a principle, there can be no resurrection without death in some form. In either case, regardless of the cause of death or suspension of function, whether the nature is spiritual or natural, resurrection involves the recovery and restoration of the original purpose.

However, what is resurrection in the faith community? What is the significance of this concept? Is resurrection in association with the next life only? Are there implications in this present existence? In this section, we shall explore the spiritual and sociological implications of the Resurrection because master churches must gain a depth of understanding often overlooked.

The genius of Christianity is that Jesus did not stop living when he died but rather dealt a fatal blow to death. And because of this resurrection event, the promise of the Father was released, and Christ is incarnate in the lives of His children. The first Adam left a legacy of death, but the last Adam left a legacy of immortality and victory. Everything about the Cross is corrective, for we are crucified to the world; sin and death are defeated; and Satan is crushed. Because of the Resurrection, we are raised together with Him, and we have victory over hell, death, and the grave. Because of the Resurrection, we are seated in heavenly places with Him, and we are His children.

Master churches will understand that a resurrection emphasis is not a minimizing of the Cross. The Resurrection infuses the crucifixion with meaning: He is triumphant. If we are to confront the world with the full scope of the Christ event, we must deal more with the Resurrection and, as a result of the Resurrection, the full release of the person of the Holy Ghost. While the Cross reveals the cost of salvation, it is the Resurrection that displays the fullness of power attained.

In examining the early Christian message of the apostles, it is clear that the focus was on the Resurrection. In our contemporary churches, altar calls are often made on the basis of the Cross while the Apostolic appeal was the Resurrection. The first evangelist proclaimed that the resurrection of Christ secured salvation, forgiveness, and the gift of the Holy Spirit. Elsewhere in the New Testament, the Gospel is associated with the Resurrection. In its broadest scope, the Gospel contains the entire Christ event and certainly the death and resurrection. But the Resurrection itself, like no other Christ event, encapsulates the Gospel. The apostles understood the meaning of Christ's death from the vantage point of the Resurrection. Apart from the Resurrection, the death of Jesus would have been an obscene tragedy. The resurrection turned night into day for the apostles. In sum, the Crucifixion speaks of the end of dimensions of spiritual life while the Resurrection initiates the beginning. In fact, the Resurrection is the authorization of Pentecost. Unless He went away, the Comforter would not have come (John 16:7).

In moving forward to modern theological writings, most material written on Christology deals with the life, ministry, miracles, and death of Jesus. In fact, the two primary emphases are the birth of Jesus and the death of Jesus. For example, Roman Catholic theology focuses on the birth of Jesus as incarnation theology and puts emphasis on Mary along with the virgin birth of Jesus. In addition, Roman Catholic theology emphasizes the death of Jesus via crucifixion, as indicated by the crucifix symbol found in all Catholic churches and in many Catholic homes. Protestant theology emphasizes the death of Jesus via crucifixion, focusing on the cross and the sacrificial blood of Jesus. Reformation emphasis was on the substitutionary sacrifice of Christ as an expiation for sin. Protestant theology has so emphasized the crucifixion that it has failed to see that only the Resurrection endowed the cross with meaning. Catholicism made the incarnation central to its theology, and Protestantism made the atonement of the cross the central thing, and as a result, neither has done justice to the apostolic emphasis on the risen life.

From these two Christian perspectives, if the incarnation and the crucifixion were the only historical acts of God on man's behalf, then the Gospel would cease to be "good news." If the Gospel narrative was that Jesus came and died for your sins, meaning "go now and sin no more," for the slate is wiped clean, then this would be a limited gospel. If the incarnation and the crucifixion were the only story, then we could not live and die as He did. We could not reproduce His impeccable life. Master churches must go beyond the initial portions of the Gospel and embrace more of the whole message and the consequences thereof.

Only in the Resurrection do we have the message that God has given us the provision of His life in order that humanity might be what God intended. The Resurrection is the positive provision of life in Christ around which all other theological topics must revolve and be oriented. It is the certification that all the events that preceded have eschatological significance and function as catalysts for the hope of the age to come. Jesus is declared to be the Son of God by the Spirit of holiness and the Resurrection.

When Christian theology has attempted to address the Resurrection in its historical consideration, it has been through apostolic arguments as a defense of the deity of Jesus and as a futuristic expectation of the bodily resurrection of believers. Christian theology has emphasized the historical significance of the Resurrection through a variety of sources to document, authenticate, and validate the historical resurrection of Jesus. Such writings by Apologists Frank Morgan ("Who Moved the Stone") and Josh McDowell ("The Resurrection Factor") have sought to provide Christians with historical "proof" of the resurrection. However, once the historical proof has been documented, then there must be some exploration of the meaning of the mystery itself, not simply to validate the church's claim about the divinity of Jesus, the authority of the church, and the possession of an exclusive truth.

The theological treatments of the Resurrection have been used to validate the assurance of the eventual resurrection of Christians' bodies in the future. The historical and bodily resurrection of Jesus is used as the foundational basis for validating the expected bodily resurrection of the Christian after death. Paul's argument in the Resurrection chapter of 1 Corinthians 15 is one such validation, but it is not the only meaning. Paul addresses the fact that believers in his day were so enamored with their present "spirituality" that they were neglecting or denying anything beyond the present. To counter this triumphalism and to correct Hellenic concept that depreciated embodiment, Paul ties the bodily resurrection of Jesus with the expected bodily resurrection of Christians. In so doing, Paul does not simply imply that the resurrected physical body of Jesus is a prototype of the resurrected body of the Christian after death.

The predominance of Paul's reference to the resurrection of Jesus is not simply to the future bodily resurrection of Christians. Paul's emphasis is that anyone who is receptive to faith in Jesus can be spiritually raised to "newness of life" (Rom.; 6:4-5) by the resurrected life of Jesus. Paul also emphasized the present availability of life in Christ.

In clear connection to the resurrection, New Testament theology emphasizes that the promises of God are now realized in Jesus Christ. Christian theology looks back to the "finished work" of Jesus (John 17:4; 19:30). This is most significant, for at times, we have focused on the Second Coming of Jesus at the expense of an emphasis on the First Coming and all that it entails. At the First Coming, a new and living way to God is provided and the works of sin are destroyed by His sacrifice and impeccable life. The Second Coming will not be for salvation, but rather for judgment. We should preach the First Coming and make reference to the Second Coming and not the reverse. It is not what is coming but that it is done. Master churches understand this emphasis and balance.

Herein is the crux of understanding and properly preaching the Resurrection: If our theology does not go beyond cradle and the cross, the birth and death of Jesus, then all we have to offer is a static history lesson with no contemporary consequences If Christian theology does not go beyond an apologetic defense of what "was" and a longing expectation of "what will be," then it becomes a constant object of our contemporary struggle for relevance and a comparison with other religions.

In summation, then, resurrection theology must also emphasize the present dynamic of life in the risen and living Lord Jesus. Such a theology will be an accurate depiction of what was previewed in the Old Testament and explained in the New Testament. Everything in the Old Testament was a prefigure for what God was going to do in the resurrection of His Son, Jesus.

The Resurrection was a replay of the Genesis account of "coming into being" for the resurrection of the last Adam presents God breathing "the spirit of life" into man again that he might become a spiritually alive soul. Mankind is regenerated and becomes a "new creation." Furthermore, resurrection is the basis of the Exodus story, bringing mankind out of the land of slavery into the promised land. Christ's coming out of the grave is seen to correspond to Moses and the people coming out of Egypt, where resurrection becomes the liberating exodus of salvation history. The history of Israel becomes the story of the Resurrection and all the prophetic promises of God are affirmed by the Resurrection. Remember that He was declared the Son of God by the Spirit of holiness and the Resurrection. Master churches will comprehend and express these truths.

CHAPTER 9

NEGLECTED EMPHASIS: The Person and Ministry of the Holy Spirit

This past century is marked with tremendous revival emphases. Beginning with the Pentecostal Movement, there follows a series of other movements that restore principles and practices previously neglected or abandoned by the Church and that reflect the finished work of Christ. The Holy Spirit has reformed our thinking on such issues as the Kingdom of God, spiritual authority, prophecy, evangelism, prayer, healing, deliverance, faith, miracles, covenant, worship, five-fold ministry, body ministry, unity, reconciliation of race and gender, and many others.

As a result of these movements, there has grown an increased awareness of the unity of the Body of Christ. Of particular interest is the fact that the Pentecostal/Charismatic dimension of the Church receives more visibility and credibility. Television, radio, conferences, and other media exposure has brought the person and ministry of the Holy Spirit into the homes, market places, and even the political world where laws and legislation are formed. As the "Spirit-filled" ministries and churches have become popular, multitudes have joined their ranks along with a host of celebrities, entertainers, politicians, professionals, and wealthy entrepreneurs. In order to manage this explosion of growth, churches have developed ministry programs, organizational structures, and beautiful buildings. In addition, rising cost factors have demanded that pastors and leaders preach more "vision-driven messages" to enlist the commitment and financial participation of their partners and members.

With such an emphasis on productivity, growth, and efficiency, a subtle anti-Charismatic sentiment has resulted in some churches. It is not expressed as an aggressive attack or censorship, but as a subtle negligence of the person of the Holy Spirit and His ministry. Once there was corporate singing of psalms, hymns, spiritual songs, and making of melodies in the hearts of believers; once there was prophetic preaching sprinkled with words of knowledge and wisdom; once there was the manifestation of faith, miracles, signs, and wonders; and once there was corporate obedience to spiritual directives regarding evangelism and witnessing to the world. But gradually, such spiritual activities have declined as the demand for more social acceptability, sophistication, and professionalism became greater. In addition to many developments in the types of ministries and expression of worship, multiple services became necessary to accommodate the growing crowds of people. As a result, congregational church time became critical, and there was not enough time to risk these creative and spontaneous expressions of the Holy Spirit. Indeed, there was and still is preaching, teaching, singing, and dancing for two or three hours on a Sunday. And there are still those scheduled "special meetings" for healing, miracles, and celebration. However, congregations and leaders who were once eager participants with the Holy Spirit began to degenerate into bands of spectators watching a religious drama. The institutionalization of the church with its mounting emphasis on structure, programs, organization, efficiency and need for more social acceptability has reduced the Holy Spirit to a doctrine, a song, a dance, or even to a "special meeting."

This analysis may seem strange at first when you consider that a casual glimpse back over the past century reveals such an increase in new ministries, churches, and outreach programs. After all, whenever Christianity becomes a living force, the doctrine of the Holy Spirit receives some primary attention. Yet, how can there be an increase in ministry activities and a decrease in recognition of the Holy Spirit as a dynamic person of the Holy Trinity? It is because during a century of restoration and the increased popularity of charismatic activities, the Holy Spirit became synonymous with the activities and all of the programs. Thus, the multitudes have been attracted to "the loaves and fishes" and have missed the personal experience with the One who makes it all possible: the Holy Spirit himself.

In fact, the term "Spirit-filled," which once was used to certify the presence of the Baptism in the Holy Spirit, has since been cast aside in favor of other trendy expressions. To be more specific, when was the last time a message was preached on the person and ministry of the Holy Spirit? Because most church growth has been accomplished, to some degree, through the transfer of memberships from one ministry to another, no one proactively seeks to know from the new members "if God gave them the same gift as He gave us when we believed on the Lord Jesus Christ" (Acts 11:17). Consequently, the activities and programs of churches became a substitute for the presence of the Holy Spirit. The Holy Spirit is a person and not a series of ministry programs. Master churches must recognize and be able to preach the Holy Spirit as a dynamic person of the Godhead, and not an ethereal cloud or some kind of self-help program or church activity benefit.

There is a very significant observation to be made here. Whenever there is a decline in personal involvement with the person and ministry of the Holy Spirit, an increase in human activities serves as a camouflage. The words of the prophet may seem to be coarse, but nonetheless true, when he declares, "Forasmuch as this people draw near me with their mouth, and with their lips do honor me, but have removed their heart far from me, and their fear toward me is taught by the precept of men" (Isaiah 29:13). Whenever there is a rise in strife, contention, division, and internal moral and ethical disintegration of ministries, there is a corresponding decline in the emphasis on the person and character of the Holy Spirit. Pentecost was the manifestation of power and character, and yet, there have been times, in the modern church congregation, when the emotional levels of parishioners did not correspond to their commitment and character levels. They were near the Lord with their mouths but their hearts were far from Him

Master churches will discern and avoid these subtle distortions. They will develop and maintain a redemptive consciousness by remembering and rehearsing the things of God. They will be mindful of these mistakes in history and not repeat them.

CHAPTER 10

COMPARING SPIRITUAL WITH SPIRITUAL

We have already expressed the proposition that the true effectiveness and relevance of churches cannot be measured by their physical structure, size of congregation, and staff. This section explores more reasons for this proposition.

The Apostle Paul introduces the idea of a "natural man" and a "spiritual man"(1 Cor. 2:11-16). This distinction rests in the salvation experience. The Apostle exhorts the Corinthians to compare spiritual things with spiritual things and compare natural things with natural things. The implication of this revelation to the church is significant. For example, the Church as redeemed people is a spiritual entity that exists in a natural world. When measuring the effectiveness and relevance of the Church, there are Divine standards that must be used. These standards are not dependent upon natural characteristics such size of congregation, nature of worship space, nor economic ability. The ability of the Church to influence the world is based upon its privilege to receive and communicate Divine information and strategies; to receive answers to prayers; and to obey the Lord. These privileges are expressed in the following factors:

*__Discernment__: knowing times and season and having the ability to

give clarity
***Foresight**: understanding the future and appropriate responses
***Persuasiveness**: having the ability to precipitate trust in their presence
***Transcendence**: having the willingness to communicate across natural borders of culture, race, age, socioeconomic and gender
***Integrity**: demonstrating charisma and character
***Spirit Dynamic**: employing the power to influence the natural
***Global Awareness**: being conscious of the world beyond the borders of religion
***Compassion**: having the skills to comfort a hurting world
***Longevity**: demonstrating persistence, endurance and effectiveness
***Consistency**: exhibiting dependability and reliability

These characteristics are expressions of the Holy Spirit working through a redeemed community of people as teacher, guide, influencer, revelator, and administrator. These are spiritual capabilities that create a community of impact and influence. These spiritual abilities are not restricted by natural characteristics such as size of congregation, nature of worship space, financial abilities, geographic location, or the communication skills and talent of the leadership.

This principle of comparing spiritual with spiritual demonstrates the reality that there can be Divine compensation for human inability in the form of favor, provision, deliverance, and grace. There is no diminishing the necessity of facilities, skills, and commitment, but there is the recognition that the "race is not to the swift, nor is the battle to the strong" (Eccl. 9:11). Furthermore, the effectiveness of the Church must be evaluated by concrete, natural standards. Master churches will understand this principle.

CHAPTER 11

REFORMATIONS, FADS AND TIMES OF REFRESHING

As we continue our discussion of master churches, it is important that there be clarity regarding times and seasons. This is particularly true when it comes to evaluating times of spiritual revivals and changes.

Reformations represent periods of change and revival of principles and practices with Biblical significance. In addition, they represent periods of corporate repentance, renewed religious zeal, large-scale evangelism, social reforms, and even miraculous demonstrations of Pentecostal power. In a reformation, the principles, precepts, and practices revived are reproducible by faith after the reformation period has ended.

REFORMATIONS

Reformations represent periods of change and revival of principles and practices with Biblical significance. In addition, they represent periods of corporate repentance, renewed religious zeal, large-scale evangelism, social reforms, and even miraculous demonstrations of Pentecostal power. In a reformation, the principles, precepts, and practices revived are reproducible by faith after the reformation period has ended.

Reformations are not restricted to a place, people or conditions. As such, they are not time-specific, situation-specific, or geography-specific. Universality is a critical characteristic of reformation. The footprint of a reformation is very broad and may cover different geographic places, times, and seasons at the same time. Generally, reformations have a sociopolitical impact in that they influence and even change the social, political and spiritual dimension of the culture. The following is a list of some historic reformation movements, their influence, and the denominational churches that arose out of their activities:

1. **Protestant** (1517 - 1648): justification by faith, repentance from dead works (Lutheran, Episcopal and Presbyterian)
2. **Evangelical** (1811 -): personal salvation, commitment to missionary work and evangelism, the Bible is inerrant, application of gospel principles to social, political, and economic issues (Reformed Episcopal, Reformed Presbyterian, New Testament Christian)
3. **Holiness** (1840 -): sanctification, faith toward God, healing, moral aspects of the law (Baptist, Methodist and Evangelical)
4. **Pentecostal** (1901 -): doctrine of baptism of the Holy Spirit that yields demonstration of spiritual gifts and power through prophecy, tongues, interpretation, hand clapping, dancing in the Spirit, shouting (Assembly of God, Pentecostal Holiness, Foursquare, Church of God)
5. **Latter Rain** (1948 -): prophecy, personal revelation, acts of faith, inspired word of knowledge and wisdom, laying on hands for healing, demonic deliverance, Holy Ghost baptism, impartation of the gifts of Spirit, praise and singing spiritual songs ushers God into worship (Charismatic and Independent)

FADS

As aforementioned, reformations present principles and practices that are reproducible by faith. They often spark revival interest in numerous areas of church life such as government, evangelism, restoration, and reconciliation. Reformations differ from fads and times of refreshing in character, redemptive value, application, and duration. Fads, for example, represent temporary intrusions into the religious or social practices, principles, policies, and standards of behavior that deviate from the status quo.

Fads are generally not universal in their application and cannot be reproduced by faith. That is, they may be limited to a specific geographic area of people. For example, clothing fads are often limited to a specific time and place, and their duration is often limited and their value not reproduceable. Spiritual fads demonstrate the same character in their emergence. For example, the emphasis on specific music, dancing, shouting, and even clothing may appear for a certain time in the worship experiences of churches but then decline.

In fact, the historical emphasis on church growth and new construction became a fad. During the 1980s, many churches began to build new sanctuaries as a sign of growth and success. While some of the construction may have been necessary, the driving force behind much of it was emulation. Churches sought to reproduce the appearance of other ministries. However, they lacked the gifting and vision of the ministries that they sought to emulate. Emulation without revelation, gifting, and calling is problematic. More importantly, to seek to reproduce other ministries without the corresponding giftings and callings generally ends in failure. It is not possible to produce a spiritual ministry without spiritual means.

TIMES OF REFRESHING

Times of refreshing are moments when charismatic activities, such as supernatural healing, deliverance, dancing in the spirit, shouting, and expressions of great joy and excitement, appear in a certain place. Generally, the experiences appear unsolicited and disappear after a period of time. Interestingly enough, their appearance was not solicited by the faith communities and could not be sustained by them nor could the experience be exported to other churches. They were sovereignly initiated and terminated, and thus, they could not be retained nor reproduced by faith.

Such experiences could be present for weeks or even months. A classic example occurred several years ago in a classical Pentecostal Church in Pensacola, Florida. The local church experienced a spontaneous explosion of miraculous events, joy, laughter, and growth. The excitement attracted thousands of visitors. The visitors experienced the refreshing while in the Pensacola church but were unable to export or reproduce the events in their local churches. The experiences were localized to that specific church and did not affect the surrounding community. While the local church was ablaze with great excitement, joy and supernatural manifestations, the local community did not benefit from any of those activities. The local community still experienced the stress of crime and social disorder while the local church carried on with its meetings day and night.

Those weeks and months of charismatic activities were restricted to the Pensacola church, and just as they spontaneously appeared, they began to decline. They could not be retained by the faith of the local church nor could they be exported by the visitors. Again, times of refreshing appear unsolicited and end unannounced. Consequently, they are not the kinds of events and experiences that should serve as a foundation for a ministry.

While miracles and manifestations of the supernatural are welcomed and should be a part of the worship experiences, a church should not build its ministry totally around such events. The teaching, preaching, and shepherding activities of the local church should continue in the presence of such experiences and even afterward. Master churches will glean from such historical experiences and discern the proper applications.

It is important to discern temporary fads and times of refreshing from principles and practices that are foundational. These fundamental principles and practices should be universal in their appearance and application, and not restricted by time, space or place. Moreover, there should be some example of such doctrines and events in the Scripture, and such experiences should be reproducible by the universal faith community. When these criteria are present, then such experiences can be considered foundational stones upon which a ministry can be established. However, activities and experiences that are not reproducible by faith and cannot be sustained by faith should not be considered foundational stones. Master churches will discern the implication and application of such times and experiences and manage them properly.

CHAPTER 12

HISTORICAL WARNINGS AND OBSERVATIONS

As we conclude our discussion on master churches, it is important to comprehend their significance in receiving and communicating Divine information. This is especially true when it comes to the mission and work of churches. Master churches will discern principles, practices, priorities, and perspectives that are indispensable for growth and progress. They will discern patterns of life and ministry that are foundational. These churches will serve as custodians of history. They will possess prophetic insight regarding the past, present and the future. This section focuses upon some observations regarding the work of churches over the years. Recommendations are made that enable us to avoid some of the same pitfalls.

1. **Imbalanced Leadership Focus**: In an evaluation of history, we can find that an overemphasis upon leadership, especially episcopal and apostolic ministry, compromised the development of the priesthood of the saints. While effective leadership is indispensable for the equipping of the saints, the emphasis on five-fold ministry and bishops directed the attention of the faith communities away from evangelism. With leadership emphasis and the focus upon structure of the churches, congregations became more leadership-dependent rather

than leadership-interdependent. While the relationship between leaders and congregations is very import, the emphasis on structure and leaders diminished the development of gifts and callings among the congregations. In essence, there was almost a silence of the priesthood of believers.

In addition, an imbalanced leadership focus upon apostles and bishops almost eclipsed the significance of the pastorate. The clamor for authority and alleged supremacy of apostles and bishops threatened to diminish the significant role of local pastors. Many local pastors became dissatisfied with their positions and sought to be "elevated" to the office of an apostle or a bishop.

Master churches understand that all ministry offices are equal in value but differ in function. Function is no criteria for value. A functional plurality that recognizes the cooperative relationship between all gifts and callings is the recommended structural relationship.

2. **Confusing Faith-Based Functions with Fads**: In the past, the emergence of religious fads and times of refreshing commanded the attention of leaders and congregations alike. As discussed in Chapter 11, there remains a great need to discern activities and patterns of thought and behavior that are Biblically based and reproduceable by faith. Foundational principles and practices can be exported, reproduced by faith and not limited to a time, place or condition. Times of refreshing were and remain spontaneous visitation of the Holy Ghost with miracles, salvation experiences, healings, deliverances, and redemptive benefits. However, such occurrences have not and may not be reproducible, and as quickly as they have appeared they would cease. Furthermore, fads were principles and practices that lacked Divine initiative and often were revival emphases being performed beyond their usefulness. Fads can still occur, and failure to discern these

distinctions have compromised the mission and work of redeemed communities.

3. **Incomplete Gospel Focus:** We must maintain that the Gospel is the power of God unto salvation. The Gospel is a comprehensive revelation that expresses the purposes, priorities, and expectations of God for the creature and creation. The Gospel reveals the comprehensive salvation process. And it must be remembered that while the salvation of the individual may be the center of His will, it is not the circumference. Salvation, then, is both individual and universal. The Gospel can be diminished and improperly divided when aspects of salvation benefits are emphasized at the expense of others. For example, there can be no focus upon the privileges and benefits of believers without stressing the responsibilities of believers in evangelism and stewardship of the world. The Gospel should reveal God in redemption as Savior and in providence as Ruler. The Gospel never divides the world into a sacred and secular sphere where Divine authority is restricted to the sacred. Influence, not escape, is the motif of the Gospel, and every legitimate dimension of human activity is affected by its power. The Gospel affords equal authority and privilege to both men and women even though a misunderstanding of terms such as "head," "helpmeet," "authority," "covering," and "submission" have been used to subjugate women. The Gospel makes clear that from one blood all nations, races, cultures, and ethnic groups emerge. All doctrines, theologies, and philosophies seeking to establish creational rights and privileges that are based upon the aforementioned distinctions are erroneous.

4. **Upending Spirit-Filled Ministry to Focus on Marketing**: The user-friendly and visitor-friendly models proved to be counter effective. While there was a need to focus upon the needs, expectations,

and values of people through statistical analyses, a genuine friendship with the Holy Spirit will always prove to generate dividends. There is indeed a need for a comfortable worship environment and the proper use of time and space to accommodate people. However, the mission and work of the Church can become subordinate to the social and environmental demands of the ministry, and that should not be. A spirit friendly environment can be created when the doctrine, practices and behavior of the Church facilitate salvation. When the congregation gathers, there should be revelation, knowledge, doctrine, prophecy, psalms, hymns, spiritual songs, ministration of gifts of the Spirit, testimonials, prayers, preaching, and teaching. There is a thin line between marketing and ministry. A Holy Spirit-friendly environment should always be generated alongside of the user-friendly and visitor-friendly model.

5. **Rejecting Close-Mindedness**: The development of relationships across theological and doctrinal boundaries is indispensable. Accommodation is not compromise. In a plural world, there is a need to recognize different and even contrary perspectives while not compromising fundamental beliefs. Transcendence means to look beyond our theological, philosophical and generational borders. The full counsel of God comes through a variety of sources. For example, a resident skeptic, not critic, can challenge our perspectives and even offer alternatives and suggestions. A confidant can provide a listening ear to our deepest concerns. A counselor can provide inspired insight during critical moments in life and ministry.

6. **Evaluating Relevancy by Divine Standards**: The evaluation of the relevance and effectiveness of ministries should be based upon Divine standards. The Kingdom of God focuses upon paradoxes that measures life and ministry upon standards other than buildings, num-

bers of people, popularity, and even geographic location. The idea of comparing spiritual things with spiritual things is a critical concept.

7. **Remembering that Divine Access Surpasses Natural Ability**: The belief that success and failure are not always a matter of ability, enthusiasm and commitment is a critical proposition. There can be Divine fortification for human inability because of the privilege to get answers to prayers and to receive and communicate Divine information. Thus, the fear of the Lord, obedience to His will, and adherence to His ways are indispensable for health and productivity of any ministry.

8. **Managing Financial Stewardship**: Financial stewardship was and can still be challenging. When people cease to give, then it is not always a financial problem but a spiritual one. There is generally a challenge to their believing apparatus. When people cease to believe because of disappointment and personal challenges, then they cease to behave. We must remember that spiritual entities, such as faith, obedience ,and confidence, express themselves in natural ways. Discernment can uncover the internal environment of a congregation, such as trust, hope, confidence, assurance, and even offenses. Moral and ethical failures among leaders create a trust crisis. This is especially true when innovative strategies are used to motivate financial giving. Investment schemes and marketing of goods and services can create significant trust issues when they are endorsed by the Church. The credibility of the Church should not rest upon the credibility of investment and marketing schemes and programs. Such programs may be used but should not be publicly endorsed by the Church.

While the church can seek other streams of income beside tithes and offerings, such programs should be carefully evaluated and managed. This is especially true of the church business model wherein the development of member businesses and entrepreneurship is stressed. To be sure, our Church stewardship does include our work and various business endeavors. And yet, all of these creative programs should be kept in context of the mission and work of the Church.

The risks and the challenges of such programs should be discussed. Special meetings can be conducted to introduce and discuss the risks, challenges, and potential dangers of such programs. The credibility of many ministries faltered because leadership did not manage financial stewardship programs properly. It is still good to ask the following questions: What is the Church? Where is the Church? When is the Church? Why is the Church?

9. **Unifying the Character of the Church**: The Body of Christ is a unified entity. Historically, churches were identified by their geographic locations such as Rome, Corinth, Colossae, Philipp, etc. They were not identified by doctrinal distinctions, such as Baptist, Pentecostal, Episcopalian, Roman Catholic, or Nondenominational. They were not labelled by ministry specifics, such as deliverance, prophetic, healing, or worship. The character of a church should express the "full counsel of God" in redemption and providence. While names of churches will rarely be changed, it would be advisable to re-examine the history behind much of these distinctions and divisions. Christ Jesus is not divided and His prayer for unity will be realized. Master churches will actively work toward unity by being aware that the Divine mandate for unity is greater than all the efforts to preserve disunity and distinction. Oneness and sameness are not synonymous. The churches can be one by reason of their redemptive origin and mandate, and yet, they can differ in their strategies and cultural identities.

10. **Relying on Technology Rather Than the Spirit**: Technology has increased the effectiveness and visibility of local churches. It has

enabled congregations to witness the gathering of churches without being in a single geographic location. That is, the creation of "cyber churches" and "virtual worship communities" has expanded the footprint of many churches. As a result, we are seeing technology and spirituality as compatible, but there is a subtle warning here. An over-dependence upon technology has compromised the sensitivity to the Holy Spirit. The Holy Spirit is the executive administrator of visions, dreams, intuition, faith, and Divine information. Sensitivity to the Holy Spirit and exercising of spiritual senses must be developed. A redemptive consciousness is a constant awareness of the indwelling presence of the Holy Spirit in each believer. It is an activation of gifts, callings, and spiritual senses in witnessing, prayer and evangelism that this consciousness is developed and exercised. While technology is a resource, it is not a substitute for spiritual interaction.

It is important for churches to see technology as a transmitter pf information, but it is not the source thereof. The luxury of "being present while being absent" through the benefits of livestreaming and other media may be compromising the spiritual development of congregations. To preserve the health and life of parishioners, hosting virtual worship services became necessary during the coronavirus pandemic, which some have called a "plague." Similarly, the invalid and chronically ill may rely upon online or televised services as a necessary substitute for their in-person attendance. However, on a normal basis, the Church must otherwise come together physically to facilitate the spiritual development and growth of the congregation. This proposition can only be accepted when the significant role and manner of the working of the Holy Spirit is understood. A ministry built around the ministry of preaching, teaching, music and dramatic presentation transmitted only through the airways will rarely reach its full potential. The integration of the presence and ministry of the Holy Spirit through gifts, callings, prayers, laying on of hands, healings, and supernatural and natural ministration demands the physical gathering of a congregation. If the corporate gathering cannot occur in one designated place, then there should be alternative gathering in smaller places such as homes and other locations.

11. **Recovering from Destructive Distinctions**: The generation gap theory that invaded churches has created significant divisions based on age. The focus upon the distinctions of age, as well as race and gender, has been a critical challenge. At times, these differences have been the basis of awarding privileges and responsibilities within ministries. Redemption restores the co-equality and co-essentiality of people regardless of age, race or gender. The re-introduction of the culture of the Kingdom of God will reform such distinctions. It may do well to refocus the teaching and preaching agendas of churches upon the realities and implications of the Kingdom of God again.

12. **Keeping Leaders Honest and Exemplary**: In being role models or influencers in any capacity, leaders must exemplify the character they champion. This is especially true in the body of believers. Those who have been entrusted to lead ministries are to adopt and exemplify the character of Christ in mind, heart and spirit. Without this, a leader's poor character could cause members of the body to fall into sin, live compromised lives or, worse, question God's love, loyalty and even His existence. Jesus warned His disciples about their behavior and the consequences of causing others to stumble because of it. It is recorded:

"And he said to his disciples, "Temptations to sin are sure to come, but woe to the one through whom they come! It would be better for him if a millstone were hung around his neck and he were cast into the sea than

that he should cause one of these little ones to sin. Pay attention to yourselves! If your brother sins, rebuke him, and if he repents, forgive him, and if he sins against you seven times in the day, and turns to you seven times, saying, 'I repent,' you must forgive him." (Matt. 18:6-9; Mark 9:42; Luke 17:1-4, ESV)

As such, master churches will have leaders who confront sin and can likewise be confronted unto repentance. These church leaders understand the seriousness of their calling and don't use their power and influence to take advantage of others in any form, including financially, sexually, psychologically or emotionally. Even ministries that proliferate with the notion of spiritual purity and scriptural integrity can fall into sin if they fail to remain guarded (Eph. 6:10-18) and truthful (John 8:32), always willing to confront, cure and cast out sin.

While these warnings and observations are not exhaustive, they embrace some critical areas of concern regarding the work and mission of churches. Master churches will provide the guidance and counsel to help avoid these pitfalls. They will serve as models to be emulated. Their influence will rest upon the privilege to get answers to prayers; to receive and communicate Divine information; and to totally obey the Lord.

May the Lord continue to revive His people and His world.

SUMMARY

What then are master churches? Fundamentally, they are Bible-based churches whose theology, sociology, structure, evangelism and worship will serve as models for other churches. While some may be megachurches with a broad ministry network, the majority of them will be smaller ministries with community impact that yields a priesthood of believers. Their effectiveness and relevance will reside in their privilege to get answers to prayers; receive and communicate Divine revelation; and to obey the Lord. Their objective will be to know the Lord and to make Him known. They will possess their own individuality based upon their geographic culture, nationality and ethnic background. The finished work of Jesus Christ and the various polarities of the Kingdom of God will greatly influence their behavior and attitude toward the world in its lost state. As aforementioned, discernment, integrity, faithfulness, endurance, love, compassion, knowledge, wisdom, faith, and consistency will be some of their identity markers. Like Noah during a time of spiritual and moral decline, these churches will receive and communicate principles, precepts, and practices that are indispensable for Biblical health and productivity within the Church.

Other Books by Clements Family Ministries

A Prevailing Spirit - a practical and insightful journey of faith and the role of traditional and alternative cures

And He Gave Them - exploring creational order and the co-equality of men and women in the home, church and market place

A Philosophy of Ministry - examines the motivation for various aspects of church ministry and programs

Spirit Friendly Church - while people-friendly programs are effective there are activities that engage the Holy Spirit

When Prophecies Fail - Exploring the source, content, intent and response of personal and end time prophecies

The Second - a look at factors that produce cooperation rather than competition in various aspects of ministry

Spiritual Intelligence - a practical guide to understanding spiritual intelligence and various factors such as knowing God and making Him known, psychic phenomena and Pentecostal power, spiritual segregation and integration and many others

Thy Kingdom Come - exploring the various concepts of the rule of God and implications upon the attitude and behavior of the believer and the church

Discernment - insightful look into discernment and the natural world of people, ideas, beliefs, and doctrines and the spiritual world of prophecies, revelations, demons and angels

Wisdom Between Pages - a book of original sayings and short statements that will provoke faith, joy, confidence and expectation

No Controversy - a short biography of the life and ministry of Sandra Clements

Navigating the Journey - an examination of the life, ministry and demise of one of the first megachurches in America, the Cathedral of the Holy Spirit

Her Name Is Mother - a practical guide to productive parenting

The Struggle and Triumph of the Believer - an examination of some of the common challenges of faith and their solutions

Order them online from various online retailers:

amazon iBooks BARNES &NOBLE

www.ingramcontent.com/pod-product-compliance
Lightning Source LLC
LaVergne TN
LVHW051159080426
835508LV00021B/2709
* 9 7 8 0 9 9 6 8 7 0 2 8 3 *